Inspiration Stori<

C000181687

THE AH-HA MOMENT

Discover What You've Been Missing This Whole Time

JUSTIN HARPER

Table of Contents

Chapter 1:

Things That Steal Your Motivation

Motivation seems a common word, sometimes a bit overrated. But it matters to those who haven't had one good moment for a long time.

The person who has everything might not like to talk about motivation. But the person who struggles and after some time gives up needs some motivation to keep going and keep doing so that he has something to achieve and live for.

Motivation is central to a good and productive life but most people lose it too soon. Some know how to regain it but some don't have a single clue what got them distracted.

Fear is a generic flaw in every human's life. People tend to fear the simplest of things and the simplest of feelings. Some call it a phobia, some call it hesitation or someone might call it smart planning.

The fact is that you don't have what it takes to do what you are reluctant to do. It may be due to fear of failure or fear of getting laughed at.

Fear keeps you from trying things that are easy to excel at and require absolutely no effort rather determination, and taking away one's determination is the direct path to demotivation

You fear something so you avoid taking a step and hence you lack the hard work that is elementary to everything in life.

Not working to your full potential is another thing that keeps the best outcomes at bay. The outcomes might surprise you and might motivate you to work even harder for the diamonds that lie ahead.

The thing that made us evolve as a human and has lead to all things we have achieved till now is competition. The competition requires us to compare our present to someone better than us and this comparison doesn't always work well for us.

We have to accept the fact that there are people more deserving and more achieved than us. But these feelings shouldn't keep us lying around and not doing to get to that place too. We have everything in life if we have a healthy body and air in our lungs. What you need more is a little motivation to get closer to the ones you idealize.

This Inferiority complex makes us wait for something to happen on its own. But what you should be doing is to get up, tie those shoes and run towards what you want. You cannot expect something to be served to you with you sitting there all day.

Chances don't come in a lottery. Fortune favors those who take risks and want to create chances. Even if you miss one chance, don't take it hard on yourself. You don't need to condemn yourself for one lost chance unless you have the same attitude when the next chance comes knocking around.

Motivation isn't a lost cause till you haven't knocked on all doors. When you have no doubts remaining, you will be successful on every next step.

Chapter 2:

Figuring Out Your Dreams

Today we're going to talk about dreams and why it is important that we all have some form of a dream or aspiration that we can work towards.

For many of us who are educated in the traditional school system, we process from one grade to the next without much thought and planning besides getting into a good school. And this autopilot has caused many kids, including myself, to not have a vision of my future and what I would like to become when I grow up. We are all taught in some shape or form that we would need to choose a career and pursue that path. Dedicating years of higher education and hundreds of hours of curriculum work only to find ourselves hating the course that we had spent all this time and energy undertaking when we step into our jobs.

This has caused many to start doubting and questioning what we ought to really do with our lives and we might get really anxious because this was certainly not part of the plan that we had set out since we were young.

What I have found personally is that I spent the time and effort to pursue a higher education not because I really wanted To, but rather to appease my parents that they did not waste all their time and money on producing me with proper schooling.

I did not however, go into my field of practice that I had spent the prior 3 years studying for. Instead upon graduating, that was when I really started to figure out what I really wanted to do with my life. Luckily for my parents, they were willing to give me the time and space to explore different possible passions and to carve out a path on my own.

I realised that as I started exploring more, and learning more about myself, the dream that I thought i once had started to change. Instead of dreaming of the perfect job and having the perfect boss, I now dreamt of freedom. To achieve freedom of time to pursue my passions, and to take steps that would move me one step closer to that dream as soon as possible.

Why this particular dream you ask? As i started exploring on successful people who have made it big in life, I realized that those that were truly happy with what they were doing, were not doing things for the money, but rather that they were able to quit their full time jobs to pursue their interests because somehow they had found a way to achieve time freedom that is irrespective of money. It amazed me how many found success by having the freedom to work from home, to not be bound by a desk job or to be hounded on my their bosses. Some live for the climb up the corporate ladder, but i knew that wasn't going to work for me. And I knew i had to make something else work to survive.

So i decided to dedicate my time and energy to only doing things that would help me achieve freedom and that became my dream to retire early and live off my past works.

The takeaway for today is that I want you to give yourself the chance to explore different things and take a step back to assess whether your current dream will actually serve you well in the long run, or if u don't even have a dream, whether you need to take time off to go find that dream for yourself.

I challenge each and everyone of you today to keep an open mind that dreams can change and you can always pursue a new path should you choose to. Because as the saying goes, the only constant in life is change.

Chapter 3:

Feeling That You Don't Have Enough Time

Today we're going to talk about a topic that I think many of us struggle with, myself included. The topic is about feeling that we don't have enough time to do the things that we need to do.

Personally I feel this one a daily basis, and it is partly because of my expectations versus reality. Many a times I set unrealistic expectations of how much time is required to do a particular task on my list that I tend to pack my schedule with way too many items. This leads me to feeling incredible overwhelm and stress because it just doesn't seem like I can get all my objectives down before 12am. We tend to underestimate the amount of time and energy that working on our goals require of us that many times we end up setting ourselves up for failure.

I would watch the clock go by minute by minute, hour by hour, only to find myself still working on the very first task on my list of 10 things to do. As you can already imagine I end up feeling that I'm not being productive, even though most of the time I am, and this feeling that I'm not doing things fast enough erodes my motivation further.

There are times when I am genuinely unproductive - like when I get lost in watching television, browsing the web, playing with my dog, being distracted for the sake of procrastination, and a myriad of reasons. But for the purposes of this topic, I will not be addressing those issues. I want to turn our attention to what we can actually accomplish if given enough time, assuming our level of productivity isnt affected by distractions.

The first thing we have to realise is that the things that we need to get done will take however long it needs to get done. Many times we may not be able to control or accurately measure the duration that a task may take. Instead of setting a time limit on a task, we should instead measure our productivity and be focused on doing rather than completing.

As an entrepreneur, I've come to learn that my work never ends. When I think I have finished one task, another one just comes crashing onto my desk like a meteor - another fire I have to put out, another problem I have to solve. I've come to realise that once I set a deadline for the time I need to complete something, rarely will I ever get it done on time. Most often I will be off by a long shot - either by the hours or even days.

Instead of setting arbitrary number of hours, I found that what worked best for me was to simply let my productivity flow. That I actually do more and accomplish more when I stop worrying about time itself - that I give my work however long it needs to get done and then call it a day.

This has allowed me to not be stressed that I never feel like I don't have enough time. Because in reality, time is relative. Time is something that I assign meaning to. If I simply focus on my designation, my 10 year plan, all I need to do is to simply work hard each day and that'll be good enough for me.

Right now the only thing that makes me feel like I don't have enough time, is when I actually waste them doing nothing meaningful. Having struggled with procrastination all my life, I've come to find out that I am not an innate workaholic. It doesn't come natural to me to want to do the work and that is what is causing me to feel like time is slipping away from me sometimes. That is something I have to continuously work on.

With regards to what you can learn from this - instead of racing against time to complete something, let the work flow out of you like water. Get into a state where productivity oozes out of you. Use a time tracking app to measure the amount of time that you have spent on working. Decide how much time you are willing to set aside to do your work and commit to that time. If 8 hours is the ideal, ensure that you clock those 8 hours and then end the day proud of yourself that you had already done what you set out to do at the start of the day. Never feel like you must do more and never beat yourself up for it. Be nicer to yourself as life is already hard enough as it is.

Another tip that I can recommend that has worked for me is to set a list of the top 3 things you want to do at the start of your day. Instead of the 10 that I did previously that caused me so much stress and anxiety, I have found that 3 is the ideal number of things that will bring us the most satisfaction and the least overwhelm when completing. If we are not able to complete those 3 big tasks, at least maybe we have done 1 or 2. We won't beat ourselves that we hadn't done those other 8 things at the back.

If on the other hand we have successfully completed all those 3 things by mid-day, we may choose to add another 3 items on our list. That way the carrot is never too far away and it is easily attainable should we want to add more.

So I challenge each and everyone of you to look into your day with a new set of lens. Set your intentions right at the start of each day and focus on productivity on a focused set of 3 items. Let the work flow out of you and let the task complete its course naturally without rushing. Remember that it will take as long as it takes and you will only bring yourself more stress if you set a deadline on it. Use it only as a tool for motivation but nothing else if you must set a deadline. Don't be too hard on yourself. Focus on the journey and don't be overly stressed out by feeling that you're always racing against time.

Chapter 4:

Feeling Lost In Life

Today we're going to talk about the topic of feeling lost in life and not knowing what to do next. I hope that by the end of this video I will be able to inspire you to start looking for ways to move forward and get out of your feeling of being stuck.

Feeling lost in life is a thing that I think many of us will go through at one point in our lives. It usually hits us like a truck when something that we have been working on for an extended period of life comes crashing to an end. Whether that be a long-term relationship, a long-held career, a lost of a family member, or a lost of anything that we have dedicated huge amounts of our time on.

This feeling of being lost usually comes to us in the most unexpected ways when we are not prepared for it. We feel lost because we are not sure what comes after. We are unsure of the unknown, a place we have never thought to think about because we never expect it to happen to us.

There were many times in my life when feeling lost seems to hit me when I least expect it - the most notable one being when started my first business and it came crashing to a halt due to some reasons which I would not go into. That abrupt end to my first business took me by surprise and I suddenly felt lost and unsure of what to do next. Instead of feeling sorry for myself however I took it as a life lesson and decided to find out what my next path was. It took me almost a year to figure that out because I had not planned for this. There was no backup plan or side business that I could pour my time in. For a while I did feel like I was swimming in an ocean with no end in sight. It was only after a long and arduous swim did I finally find some dry land where I could set up camp again.

For those of us who have spent most of our early years working towards a degree that we think might be the end all be all career for us, we may find ourselves completely lost at sea as well when we find that our career no longer brings us joy but dread. Or that we find ourselves completely unsuited for this career and are nearing the end of its tolerance for the job. Or that we may suddenly be fired from our positions without warning. All these factors would be natural warrants for feeling lost because we have set the expectation to only work on this job and this job alone with no backup plan whatsoever. We may realise that we had not planned to pick up any new skills that would make us attractive for hire in another career, or that we may have no idea at all of what to do next.

Feeling lost in life, whatever the reasons may be, can be avoided if we think ahead far enough into the future. When we know the kind of life that we want to lead, the kind of income that we want to earn, we can be better prepared to make decisions today that would not land us in positions where a sudden loss of job will allow us to be thrown into the deep end of the pool. If we start to feel that something is amiss in our career, we may want to start doing some research early to see what other careers we may be able to plan for should we decide to quit our jobs. For most of us, we never want to find ourselves in a place where we have no career, no job, or no income. This sets off a wave of panic and fear in us that can lead us to feeling more lost and confused in life.

I believe the best way to avoid feeling lost is to never think of anything we have as permanent. We should not expect that the same job, career, or even person will be with us forever. We may want to consider starting a side stream of income so that we do not lay all our eggs in one basket. If something were to happen to our day jobs at least we can focus on our side business to tide us over until we can figure out what else to do next.

I have applied the same principle to all aspects of my life to avoid myself feeling lost. I have made it a point to have at least 5 areas that I could potentially work on should one or more than one fail. I never want to be in a position where my day job equals my livelihood. In that way I am forever bounded by 1 career and the fear of leaving or letting go would always be too great, not to mention the uncertainty in even keeping that one job in the first place.

Relationship wise and with dealing with loss and feeling lost without someone, of course I don't recommend you to have back-ups for those. I'm not into teaching polygamy or what not. In that sense it is absolutely and perfectly normal for us to simply go through the grieving process and hopefully move on with life. We may not be able to prepare for this but it could still happen to us. Remember that you should be self-sufficient first and foremost and that sometimes we may only be able to count on ourselves. We can't guarantee that the person we choose to love will be with us forever but we can only hope for that to be true.

So I challenge each and everyone of you to look ahead of you can. Always plan for failure and remember nothing ever stays the same. Do try to be prepared if somethings does not work out and shift your attention quickly to the next project especially with career and finance. As much as you can, don't ruminate on the loss but focus on the big picture. Hopefully with all these strategies I am able to help you not fall into the same trap as I did in feeling lost in life, that you will be better equipped to handle such shocking events.

Chapter 5:

Enjoying The Simple Things

Today we're going to talk about a topic that might sound cheesy, but trust me it's worth taking a closer look at. And that is how we should strive to enjoy the simple things in life.

Many of us think we need a jam packed schedule for the week, month, or year, to tell us that we are leading a very productive and purposeful life. We find ways to fill our time with a hundred different activities. Going to this event, that event, never slowing down. And we find ourselves maybe slightly burnt out by the end of it.

We forget that sometimes simplicity is better than complication. Have you sat down with your family for a simple lunch meal lately? You don't have to talk, you just have to be in each other's company and enjoying the food that is being served in front of you.

I found myself appreciating these moments more than I did running around to activities thinking that I needed something big to be worth my time. I found sitting next to my family on the couch watching my own shows while they watch theirs very rewarding. I found eating alone at my favourite restaurant while watching my favourite sitcom to be equally as enjoyable as hanging out with a group of 10 friends. I also found myself richly enjoying a long warm shower every morning and evening. It is the highlights of my day.

My point is that we need to start looking at the small things we can do each day that will bring us joy. Things that are within our control. Things that we know can hardly go wrong. This will provide some stability to gain some pleasure from. The little nuggets in the day that will not be determined by external factors such as the weather, friends bailing on us, or irritating customers.

When we focus on the little things, we make life that much better to live through.

Chapter 6:

First Impressions Matter

Today we're going to talk about a simple topic that I hope will help each and every one of you make a good first impression in every meeting you may encounter in the future.

So why bother with making a good first impression in the first place? The answer is fairly simple - people decide very quickly in the first few minutes whether they think you are someone they might want to associate themselves with or not. They see how you look, how you dress, how you carry yourself, and they decide usually fairly quickly about what label they want to tag on you. Humans are judgemental and superficial creatures by nature. Barring all other aspects of your personality, how you look is the first thing that others can deduce about you.

We have all done this at some point in our lives - we make sweeping remarks about the first "hot guy" or "hot girl" that we see, and we we remark at the way they dress and the choices that they make stylistically. We may find ourself immediately attracted to them based on just their looks.

Of course how we carry ourselves is equally important as well. When we go for interviews, when we meet new clients, the vibes that we let out matters. How others perceive us in that first meeting will set the tone on whether we may be asked back for a second interview, or if our clients will continue to decide on whether to work with us moving forward. Sure if we don't do well in the first impression we may have a chance to redeem ourselves in the second chance we get, but I'm sure that's not where you want to end up if given the choice.

So how can we do our best to make a good first impression in any situation?

I want to start by making sure that you know who your audience is. Do your homework and try your best to anticipate what the opposing party might aspect of you. If you are going for a job interview and you know it will be a formal one, do your best to look smart and dress accordingly. Don't show up with your shirts untucked and un-ironed. Ensure that you look the part of the job you are gunning for. Sure things may go wrong during the interview, but at least you showed up looking like you really are serious about the job and that you want to look presentable for your future boss.

If you know that you are going on a first date for example, make a good first impression by also grooming yourself accordingly to attract your partner. I know it may sound incredibly superficial, but if you look into nature, almost all creatures have a way of attracting their mates. Whether it be through colourful feathers in a peacock, or dance rituals in some exotic birds, or a flowing mane of a lion, all these are ways to catch the attention of their potential partners. When someone dresses nicely it shows that they are making an effort to look good and that they are in the business of winning you over.

Now that I've given you some examples of how looking the part can give you a huge boost in your first impressions rating, I want to move on to the next part which is how you actually carry yourself through the things that you say and the actions that you take.

Everyone knows that a pretty face can only carry you so far if you don't have a good personality to match. Sure we may lust for something that looks good on the outside, but if we take a bite from it and it tastes absolutely gastly, I'm sure most of us would eventually run for the hills afterward. The same goes when you go for interviews as well.

The simplest advice I can give for all of you is to be yourself. Don't try to be something that you are not. In most situations, I believe that staying true to who you are and being congruent in what you say is very important. Yes you have to be professional and do your best to showcase your talents in your area of expertise, but beyond that we do need to try our best to be as authentic as possible. Depending on what our motives are and what we want to get out of the first impression meeting, we have to be really clear about our intentions. If our goal is to deceive, you may find it easy to lie our way through the first meeting, but the truth eventually catches up with us when the opposite party finds that we are not up for job or up to the standards that we have set for ourselves in the first session. If we had stayed true to ourselves from the very beginning, our words will hold more credit and questions to our integrity will be kept to a minimal.

If we want to attract a spouse that is kind-hearted and good-willed, it is only natural for us to expect the same if the opposing party gave us the impression that they are. If it was done out of deceit, over time it will slowly creep up as their authenticity stays to crack and we are revealed their true nature. If we expect others to act and behave the way that is congruent with what they show us in the first impression, we should also do the same for others.

Yes I know that I may be going off a tangent of creating good first impressions. But I am also not going to advocate here that we change ourself completely to make a good impression the first time around only to show up like totally different versions of ourselves the next. I always believe that staying true to who you are is the best way to not only make a good first impression, but also to make a lasting and permanent impression. We want to build a strong reputation for ourselves as individuals who are confident and competent at the same time. We want to earn others' trust not out of deceit but out of skill.

If we find ourselves lacking in certain areas, I propose that we work on it on a consistent and daily basis. If we find that maybe we're not happy with the way we look, make a commitment to get to the gym 5 times a week and to eat healthier. If we find ourselves lacking in key soft skills, we may want to take up a course or go for trainings that help us be better in these areas. If we find ourselves lacking in certain skill sets required for particular job that we want, we may want to consider getting further education so that we are qualified in those areas. The bottom line is, we should never stop working on ourselves. Only then can we truly make a powerful first impression that is credible and lasting.

So I challenge each and everyone of you today to make it a point to put making a good genuine first impression at the top of our list for every new person that we meet. Whatever the reason may be, dress up accordingly and present ourselves well so that we may hopefully get the thing that we want.

Chapter 7:

Happy People Choose to Exercise

There is a feeling you get when you just finish your workout, and you feel amazing, much better than you were feeling before. Even when you are not feeling motivated to go to the gym, just thinking about this feeling makes you get up, leave your bed and get going to the gym. This feeling can also be called an endorphin rush. Exercise indeed makes you happier in multiple ways.

Firstly, movement helps you bond with others that are in the brain chemistry of it all. Your heart rate is going up, you are using your body, engaging your muscles, your brain chemistry will change, and it will make it easier for you to connect and bond with other people. It also changes how your trust people. Research also showed that social pressures like a hug, laughing, or high-five are also enhanced. You will also find your new fitness fam, the people you will be working out with, and because you will have a shared interest that is having a healthy lifestyle will help you have a stronger bond with them. And as experts say that having strong relationships and connections in life will help you in overall happiness.

We have already discussed those exercise increases endorphins but what you do not know is that it increases a lot more brain chemicals that make you feel happy and good about yourself. Some of the brain chemicals that increase are; dopamine, endorphins, endocannabinoid and adrenaline. All of these chemicals are associated with feeling confident, capable, and happy. The amount of stress, physical pain, and anxiety also decrease significantly. A chemical that your body creates when your muscles contract is called "myokine", it is also shown to boost happiness and relieve stress.

Secondly, exercise can help boost your confidence, and of course, when it comes to feeling empowered and happy, confidence is the key. "At the point when you move with others, it's anything but a solid feeling of 'greater than self' probability that causes individuals to feel more idealistic and enabled, "Also, it permits individuals to feel more engaged turning around the difficulties in their own lives. What's more, that is a fascinating side advantage of moving with others because there's an encapsulated feeling of 'we're in the same boat' that converts into self-assurance and the capacity to take on difficulties in your day; to day existence."

Thirdly, exercising outdoors affects your brain, similar to meditation. In case you're similar to the innumerable other people who have found out about the advantages of contemplation yet can't make the time, uplifting news. You may not need to contemplate to get a portion of the advantages. Researchers found that exercising outside can similarly affect the cerebrum and disposition as reflection. Exercising outside immediately affects a state of mind that is amazingly incredible for wretchedness and nervousness. Since it's anything but a state in your mind that is the same as contemplation, the condition of open mindfulness,"

Chapter 8:

Focus On The Work You Need To Do Today

Today we're going to talk about the topic focus, and not just that, but to be very precise on exactly what you need to do each and everyday from the very beginning.

It is easy for us to get lost in the sea of things we need to do each day. From work carried over from yesterday, to the commitments that have made for the brand new day, we can forget what our priorities are over time. It is all too easy to get busy and feeling like you're being productive only to come out of it realising that you hadn't really done anything at all. Or rather that you haven't been doing the things that really matter that will move the needle forward for you in life.

When you are unclear about what you need to do, it can be all too easy to focus on the wrong things from the moment you wake up. Maybe you forgot that you need to work on your side business that you hope would one day bring you the time freedom that you crave. Maybe you forgot that you were supposed to study for that real estate exam that is supposed to help you bring some passive income while you work on your day job. Maybe you forgot that you needed to work on yourself, to become a better person so that you can be a better father, mother, parent, lover, spouse, partner, whatever your role may be. It can become all too easy to get busy with chatting with your friends on messaging apps or busy with rearranging your house or tidying up and decluttering, that the day gets away from you in the blink of an eye.

Remember that you only have one life to live and everyday is incredibly precious that should not be wasted. For every minute that you waste, they turn into hour, days, months, and before you know it, years and decades later you haven't even begun on the tasks that truly matter in life.

Before we go on I want you again to think about the areas in your life that you said you wanted to focus on. The really important things. The ones that will change your future for the better and the ones that will bring you to whatever you define as success in life. Only when we know exactly what we want can we carve out a plan of action that will take us there.

These areas that you want to pay attention could be your health for example, and you might want to start by choosing the right foods for your first meal every morning. Another area that you might want to focus on could be fitness. Take that first hour of your day to do some workouts that will improve your metabolism so that in your 50s you might still have a healthy body to enjoy the fruits of your labour. In the area of career and finance, you may want to start applying to jobs that are in line with your purpose, or maybe you might want to keep researching on ways to make more money to support you and your family. If the area you want to focus on is family, maybe the first thing you want to do instead is to spend some quality time with them. If your goal is to develop a strong and lasting bond with your wife and kids, you might want to consider carving out a certain amount of time to be with them so that you don't go by years later and realise you were never really present for your family at all. Work and money can be secondary when we realize that love is what really matters. And if your focus is your current job, stop wasting time and start cracking on that project asap. If you feel like you need to work on yourself, you might consider spending an hour every morning reading a self-help book that hopefully helps you grow your personality, or maybe watch a YouTube video like this one that teaches you how to be a better person.

The idea here is that there is no one template for everybody. You are your own person and your area of focus is unique. Only you know where you need to work on and only you know the plan of action you need to take if you want to see true and lasting change.

So I challenge each and everyone of you to clearly define the areas of your life that needs your most attention. Drill down on it each and every day. Don't stop putting the pedal on the gas in these areas. Occasionally it's okay to wander off course but always find your way back on the horse. 90% of your time should be spent on these areas with total focus. Don't let distraction and passiveness rob you of your time. Also choose to spend time on learning and growing yourself each day and the benefits will be immense.

Chapter 9:

How To Find Motivation

Today we're going to talk about a topic that hopefully will help you find the strength and energy to do the work that you've told yourself you've wanted or needed to but always struggle to find the one thing that enables you to get started and keep going. We are going to help you find motivation.

In this video, I am going to break down the type of tasks that require motivation into 2 distinct categories. Health and fitness, and work. As I believe that these are the areas where most of you struggle to stay motivated. With regards to family, relationships, and other areas, i dont think motivation is a real problem there.

For all of you who are struggling to motivate yourself to do things you've been putting off, for example getting fit, going to the gym, motivation to stay on a diet, to keep working hard on that project, to study for your exams, to do the chores, or to keep working on your dreams... All these difficult things require a huge amount of energy from us day in and day out to be consistent and to do the work.

I know... it can be incredibly difficult. Having experienced these ups and downs in my own struggle with motivation, it always starts off swimmingly... When we set a new year's resolution, it is always easy to think that we will stick to our goal in the beginning. We are super motivated to go do the gym to lose those pounds, and we go every single day for about a week... only to give up shortly after because we either don't see results, or we just find it too difficult to keep up with the regime.

Same goes for starting a new diet... We commit to doing these things for about a week, but realize that we just simply don't like the process and we give up as well...

Finding motivation to study for an important exam or working hard on work projects are a different kind of animal. As these are things that have a deadline. A sense of urgency that if we do not achieve our desired result, we might fail or get fired from our company. With these types of tasks, most of us are driven by fear, and fear becomes our motivator... which is also not healthy for us as stress hormones builds within us as we operate that way, and we our health pays for it.

Let's start with tackling the first set of tasks that requires motivation. And i would classify this at the health and fitness level. Dieting, exercise, going to the gym, eating healthily, paying attention to your sleep... All these things are very important, but not necessarily urgent to many of us. The deadline we set for ourselves to achieve these health goals are arbitrary. Based on the images we see of models, or people who seem pretty fit around us, we set an unrealistic deadline for ourselves to achieve those body goals. But more often than not, body changes don't happen in days or weeks for most of us by the way we train. It could take up to months or years... For those celebrities and fitness models you see on Instagram or movies, they train almost all day by personal trainers. And their deadline is to look good by the start of shooting for the movie. For most of us who have day jobs, or don't train as hard, it is unrealistic to expect we can achieve that body in the same amount of time. If we only set aside 1 hour a day to exercise, while we may get gradually fitter, we shouldn't expect that amazing transformation to happen so quickly. It is why so many of us set ourselves up for failure.

To truly be motivated to keep to your health and fitness goals, we need to first define the reasons WHY we even want to achieve these results in the first place. Is it to prove to yourself that you have discipline? Is it to look good for your wedding photoshoot? Is it for long term health and fitness? Is it so that you don't end up like your relatives who passed too soon because of their poor health choices? Is it to make yourself more attractive so that you can find a man or woman in your life? Or is it just so that you can live a long and healthy life, free of medical complications that plague most seniors by the time they hit their 60s and 70s? What are YOUR reasons WHY you want to keep fit? Only after you know these reasons, will you be able to truly set a realistic deadline for your health goals. For those that are in it for a better health overall until their ripe old age, you will realize that this health goal is a life long thing. That you need to treat it as a journey that will take years and decades. And small changes each day will add up. Your motivator is not to go to the gym 10 hours a day for a week, but to eat healthily consistently and exercise regularly every single day so that you will still look and feel good 10, 20, 30, 50 years, down the road.

And for those that need an additional boost to motivate you to keep the course, I want you to find an accountability partner. A friend that will keep you in check. And hopefully a friend that also has the same health and fitness goals as you do. Having this person will help remind you not to let yourself and this person down. Their presence will hopefully motivate you to not let your guard down, and their honesty in pointing out that you've been slacking will keep you in check constantly that you will do as you say.

And if you still require an additional boost on top of that, I suggest you print and paste a photo of the body that you want to achieve and the idol that you wish to emulate in terms of having a good health and fitness on a board where you can see every single day. And write down your reasons why beside it. That way, you will be motivated everytime you walk past this board to keep to your goals always.

Now lets move on to study and work related tasks. For those with a fixed 9-5 job and deadlines for projects and school related work, your primary motivator right now is fear. Which as we established earlier, is not exactly healthy. What we want to do now is to change these into more positive motivators. Instead of thinking of the consequences of not doing the task, think of the rewards you would get if you completed it early. Think of the relief you will feel knowing that you had not put off the work until the last minute. And think of the benefits that you will gain... less stress, more time for play, more time with your family, less worry that you have to cram all the work at the last possible minute, and think of the good results you will get, the opportunities that you will have seized, not feeling guilty about procrastinations... and any other good stuff that you can think of. You could also reward yourself with a treat or two for completing the task early. For example buying your favourite food, dessert, or even gadgets. All these will be positive motivators that will help you get the ball moving quicker so that you can get to those rewards sooner. Because who likes to wait to have fun anyway?

Now I will move on to talk to those who maybe do not have a deadline set by a boss or teacher, but have decided to embark on a new journey by themselves. Whether it be starting a new business, getting your accounting done, starting a new part time venture.. For many of these tasks, the only motivator is yourself. There is no one breathing down your neck to get the job done fast and that could be a problem in itself. What should we do in that situation? I believe with this, it is similar to how we motivate ourselves in the heath and fitness goals. You see, sheer force doesn't always work sometimes. We need to establish the reasons why we want to get all these things done early in life. Would it be to fulfil a dream that we always had since we were a kid? Would it be to earn an extra side income to travel the world? Would it be to prove to yourself that you can have multiple streams of income? Would it to become an accomplished professional in a new field? Only you can define your reasons WHY you want to even begin and stay on this new path in the first place. So only you can determine why and how you can stay on the course to eventually achieve it in the end.

Similarly for those of you who need additional help, I would highly recommend you to get an accountability partner. Find someone who is in similar shoes as you are, whether you are an entrepreneur, or self-employed, or freelance, find someone who can keep you in check, who knows exactly what you are going through, and you can be each other's pillars of support when one of you finds yourself down and out. Or needs a little pick me up. There is a strong motivator there for you to keep you on course during the rough time.

And similar to health and fitness goal, find an image on the web that resonates with the goal you are trying to achieve. Whether it might be to buy a new house, or to become successful, i want that image to always be available to you to look at every single day. That you never forget WHY you began the journey. This constant reminder should light a fire in you each and everyday to get you out of your mental block and to motivate you to take action consistently every single day.

So I challenge each and every one of you to find motivation in your own unique way. Every one of you have a different story to tell, are on different paths, and no two motivators for a person are the same. Go find that one thing that would ignite a fire on your bottom everytime you look at it. Never forget the dream and keep staying the course until you reach the summit.

Chapter 10:

Do You Know What You Want?

Do you know who you are? Do you know what you are? Do you know what you want to become? Do you have any idea what you might become?

Every sane human has asked these questions to themselves multiple times in their lives. We have a specific trait of always finding the right answers to everything. We humans always try to find the meaning behind everything.

It's in our built-in nature to question everything around us. Yet we are here in this modern era of technology and resources and we don't have a sense of purpose. We don't have a true set of goals. We don't give enough importance to our future to take a second and make a long-term plan for longer gains.

The fault in our thinking is that we don't have a strict model of attention. We have too many distractions in our lives to spare a moment to clear our minds.

The other thing that makes us confused or ignorant is the fact that people have a way of leading us into thinking things that are not ours to start with.

Society has made these norms that have absolutely nothing to do with anyone except that these were someone's experience when they were once at our stage. We are dictated on things that are not ours to achieve but only a mere image of what others want us to achieve or don't.

No one has the right to tell you anything. No one has a right to say anything to you except if they are advising or reminding you of the worst. But to inflict a scenario with such surety that it will eventually happen to you because you have a fault that many others had before you is the most superstitious and illogical thing to do on any planet let alone Earth. No one knows what the future holds for anyone. No one can guarantee even the next breath that they take. So why put yourself under someone else's spell of disappointment? Why do you feel the need to satisfy every person's whim? Why do you feel content with everyone around you getting their ways?

You always know in your heart, deep down in some corner what you want. You will always know what you need to be fulfilled. You will always find an inspiration within yourself to go and pursue that thing. What you need are some self-confidence and some self-motivation. You need to give yourself some time to straighten up your thoughts and you will eventually get the BOLD statement stating 'This is what I want'.

You don't need to shut everyone around you. You just need to fix your priorities and you will get a vivid image of what things are and what they can become.

There is no constraint of age or gender to achieving anything. These are just mental and emotional hurdles that we have imposed on our whole race throughout our history.

Just remember. When you know what you want, and you want it bad enough to give away everything for that, you will someday find a way to finally get it.

Chapter 11:

Being Open To Opportunities For Social Events

As we continue from the previous video, something I learned is that things never turn out as how you would expect to in life. And the more we try to force something, the more resistance we face. And the more we take things in stride and just trust the process, the more things tend to flow naturally. You will see what I mean as we go through this video together.

As I was describing about how my social life was basically non existent at one point, if you guys haven't watched that video, do check it out first.

After taking a hard look at the decisions I made that left me with little to no social support or events to go to, i knew that I needed to do a 180 if i hoped to see any sort of rebound in my social life. And I started making a concrete plan with specific actions that would put me in a favourable position to attract and keep new friends.

At my lowest point, I knew that there was little that I could do to salvage my previous relationships, that I had probably done irreparable harm to them and i needed to start all over again. And that is to Make new friends from scratch. It wasn't so much something that I felt i needed right away, but i knew that in the long run, investing in friendships would bring me much more joy than money ever could especially in the latter years of my life. I knew that money wasn't the end all be all, and that people was the way to go.

Money can be made, but friendships cannot be bought.

I started the goal of dedicating this year and beyond to new friendships and began by signing up for activities that were in line with my interests. As an avid tennis fan and a player of the game, i decided that that was where i would begin. I started joining tennis groups and started playing games with complete strangers. Having also a growing interest in yoga and working out, I also started going for classes with my membership. Whilst i did not really make any real friends right away, I felt that I was already connected in some ways to people with similar interests. And I felt like i was part of a community, that I belonged somewhere. The more i showed up for these activities, the more people kept seeing me around, and the more these people started associated me as being regulars. Soon I was invited by one or two people to join a private game and that in itself became a regular thing. I started seeing these faces weekly for a year and we became friends naturally over the game of tennis. Yoga was a different story as it was more of an individual kind of sport, and people were generally more focused on their own practice on the mat, but it was fine as my interest for yoga faded pretty quickly anyway.

At the gym I started making one or two friends as well. It became natural to chat up with the gym regulars and even the staff, i felt like i looked forward to attending these events not because I wanted to work out, but because I enjoyed the social part and meeting my new friends and striking up random conversations.

For those of you who work in 9-5 jobs, you might not face this same issue as me, as meeting new people and colleagues would be a very simple way to start making new aquaintances that could potentially turn into friends... Seeing that you would meet them every single day whether you liked it or not. But for people who work from home or who are self employed, we do need to make the extra effort to meet new people.

As my pool of friends grew bigger, I started forming my own private tennis group, putting in the extra effort to book the courts day in and out, and inviting them to play. Eventually all my hard work paid off, as people reciprocated by inviting me to their own private outings and dinners. And I started to integrate into their lives and their friends. I had made myself so readily available, not by design, but by choice because at that point I was so ready to say yes to anything it became so natural to prioritise hanging out over just simply working all day and night. My friends saw me as someone they could count on to be there and they had no qualms making me a priority when they wanted to find somebody to hang out with. I reciprocated by making them a priority as well. And the friendship blossomed from there.

For the first time in a long time, I felt truly alive. I felt that my life had a purpose, it had balance, it had work and play, there was yin to my yang, and i looked forward to working as much as I looked forward to hanging out.

I don't know how long this bliss will last, but i know that I had made the right choice. This all happened in 2020, smack in the middle of the pandemic, and yet I made it work because I had given myself every opportunity to succeed.

If this story resonated with you, then i challenge each and everyone of you today to simply decide on a time and place you would like to begin changing the areas of your life that you find lacking. The one thing that I have learned from all this is that it is never tooo late to turn things around. Whether it be financial, emotional, or physical. A firm decision to change is all it takes. And giving it time to grow and blossom is essential to seeing long term success.

I hope you have learned something today and I wish you all the best in putting yourself in positions where opportunities would arise.

Chapter 12:

Deal With Your Fears Now

Fear is a strange thing.

Most of our fears are phantoms that never actually appear or become real,

Yet it holds such power over us that it stops us from making steps forward in our lives.

It is important to deal with fear as it not only holds you back but also keeps you caged in irrational limitations.

Your life is formed by what you think.

It is important not to dwell or worry about anything negative.

Don't sweat the small stuff, and it's all small stuff (Richard Carlson).

It's a good attitude to have when avoiding fear.

Fear can be used as a motivator for yourself.

If you're in your 30s, you will be in your 80s in 50 years, then it will be too late.

And that doesn't mean you will even have 50 years. Anything could happen.

But let's say you do, that's 50 years to make it and enjoy it.

But to enjoy it while you are still likely to be healthy, you have a maximum of 15 years to make it - minus sleep and living you are down to 3 years.

If however you are in your 40s, you better get a move on quickly.

Does that fear not dwarf any possible fears you may have about taking action now?
Dealing with other fears becomes easy when the ticking clock is staring you in the face.
Most other fears are often irrational.

We are only born with two fears, the fear of falling and the fear of load noises.
The rest have been forced on us by environment or made up in our own minds.
The biggest percentage of fear never actually happens.

To overcome fear we must stare it in the face and walk through it knowing our success is at the other side.
Fear is a dream killer and often stops people from even trying.
Whenever you feel fear and think of quitting, imagine behind you is the ultimate fear of the clock ticking away your life.

If you stop you lose and the clock is a bigger monster than any fear.
If you let anything stop you the clock will catch you.

So stop letting these small phantoms prevent you from living,
They are stealing your seconds, minutes, hours , days and weeks.
If you carry on being scared, they will take your months, years and decades.

Before you know it they have stolen your life.

You are stronger than fear but you must display true strength that fear will be scared.
It will retreat from your path forever if you move in force towards it because fear is fear and by definition is scared.

We as humans are the scariest monsters on planet Earth.
So we should have nothing to fear
Fear tries to stop us from doing our life's work and that is unacceptable.
We must view life's fears as the imposters they are, mere illusions in our mind trying to control us.

We are in control here.
We have the free will to do it anyway despite fear.
Take control and fear will wither and disappear as if it was never here.
The control was always yours you just let fear steer you off your path.

Fear of failure, fear of success, fear of what people will think.
All irrational illusions.
All that matters is what you believe.
If your belief and faith in yourself is strong , fear will be no match for your will.

Les Brown describes fear as false evidence appearing real.
I've never seen a description so accurate.

Whenever fear rears its ugly head, just say to yourself this is false evidence appearing real.

Overcoming fear takes courage and strength in one's self.
We must develop more persistence than the resistance we will face when pursuing our dreams.
If we do not develop a thick skin and unwavering persistence we will be beaten by fear, loss and pain.

Our why must be so important that these imposters become small in comparison.
Because after all the life we want to live does dwarf any fears or set back that might be on the path.
Fear is insignificant.
Fear is just one thing of many we must beat into the ground to prove our worth.
Just another test that we must pass to gain our success.

Because success isn't your right,
You must fight
With all your grit and might
Make it through the night and shine your massive light on the world.
And show everyone you are a star.

Chapter 13:

Being 100% Happy Is Overrated

Lately I've been feeling as though happiness isn't something that truly lasts. Happiness isn't something that will stay with us very long. We may feel happy when we are hanging out with friends, but that feeling will eventually end once we part for the day. I've been feeling as though expecting to be constantly happy is very overrated. We try to chase this idea of being happy. We chase the material possessions, we chase the fancy cars, house, and whatever other stuff that we think will make us happy. But more often than not the desire is never really fulfilled. Instead, i believe that the feeling accomplishment is a much better state of mind to work towards. Things will never make us happy. We may enjoy the product we have worked so hard for temporarily. But that feeling soon goes away. And we are left wondering what is the next best thing we can aim our sights on. This never-ending chase becomes a repetitive cycle, one that we never truly are aware of but constantly desire. We fall into the trap that finding happiness is the end all-be-all.

What i've come to realise is that most of the time, we are actually operating on a more baseline level. A state that is skewed more towards the neutral end. Neither truly happy, or neither truly sad. And I believe that is perfectly okay. We should allow ourselves to embrace and accept the fact that it is okay to be just fine. Just neutral. Sure it isn't something very exciting, but we shouldn't put ourselves in a place where we expect to be constantly happy in order to lead a successful life. This revelation came when I realised that every time I felt happy, I would experience a crash in mood the next day. I would start looking at instagram, checking up on my friends, comparing their days, and thinking that they are leading a happier life than I was. I would then start berating myself and find ways to re-create those happy moments just for the sake of it. Just because I thought i needed to feel happy all the time. It was only when I actually sat down and started looking inwards did I realise that maybe I can never truly find happiness from external sources.

Instead of trying to find happiness in things and external factors that are beyond my control, I started looking for happiness from within myself. I began to appreciate how happy I was simply being alone. Being by myself. Not letting other factors pull me down. I found that I was actually happiest when I was taking a long shower, listening to my own thoughts. No music playing, no talking to people, just me typing away on my computer, writing down all the feelings I am feeling, all the thoughts that I am thinking, letting every emotion I was feeling out of my system. I started to realise that the lack of distractions, noise, comparisons with others, free from social media, actually provided me with a clearer mind. It was in those brief moments where I found myself to be my most productive, with ideas streaming all over the place. It was in that state of mind that I did feel somewhat happy. That I could create that state of mind without depending on other people to fulfil it for me.

If any of you out there feel that your emotions are all over the place, maybe it is time for you to sit down by yourself for a little while. Stop searching for happiness in things and stuff, and sometimes even people. We think it is another person's job to make us happy. We expect to receive compliments, flowers, a kiss, in order to feel happy. While those things are certainly nice to have, being able to find happiness from within is much better. By sitting and reflecting in a quiet space, free from any noise and distractions, we may soon realise that maybe we are okay being just okay. Maybe we don't need expensive jewellery or handbags or fancy houses to make us happy. Maybe we just need a quiet mind and a grateful spirit.

The goal is to find inner peace. To accept life for the way it is. To accept things as the way they are. To be grateful for the things we have. That is what it means to be happy.

Chapter 14:

Discomfort Is Temporary

It's easy to get hopeless when things get a little overwhelming. It's easy to give up because you feel you don't have the strength or resources to continue. But where you stop is actually the start you have been looking for since the beginning.

Do you know what you should do when you are broken? You should relish it. You should use it. Because if you know you are broken, congratulations, you have found your limitations.

Now as you know what stopped you last time, you can work towards mending it. You can start to reinforce the breach and you should be able to fill in the cracks in no time.

Life never repeats everything. One day you feel the lowest and the next might bring you the most unpredictable gifts.

The world isn't all sunshine and rainbows. It is a very mean and nasty place to be in. But what can you do now when you are in it? Nothing? Never!

You have to endure the pain, the stress, the discomfort till you are comfortable with the discomfort. It doesn't make any sense, right? But listen to me.

You have a duty towards yourself. You have a duty towards your loved ones. You are expected to rise above all odds and be something no one has ever been before you. I know it might be a little too much to ask for, but, you have to understand your purpose.

Your purpose isn't just to sit on your back and the opportunities and blessings keep coming, knocking at your door, just so you can give up one more time and turn them down.

Things are too easy to reject and neglect but always get hard when you finally step up and go for them. But remember, every breathtaking view is from the top of a hill, but the trek to the top is always tiring. But when you get to the top, you find every cramp worth it.

If you are willing to put yourself through anything, discomfort and temporary small intervals of pain won't affect you in any way. As long as you believe that the experience will bring you to a new level.

If you are interested in the unknown, then you have to break barriers and cross your limits. Because every path that leads to success is full of them. But then and only then you will find yourself in a place where you are unbreakable.

You need to realize that your life is better than most people out there. You need to embrace the pain because all this is temporary. But when you are finally ready to embrace the pain, you are already on your way to a superior being.

Life is all about taking stands because we all get all kinds of blows. But we always need to dig in and keep fighting till we have found the gems or have found our last breath.

The pain and discomfort will subside one day, but if you quit, then you are already on the end of your rope.

Chapter 15:

Creating Successful Habits

Successful people have successful habits.

If you're stuck in life, feeling like you're not going anywhere, take a hard look at your habits.

Success is built from our small daily habits accumulated together,

Without these building blocks, you will not get far in life.

Precise time management, attention to detail, these are the traits of all who have made it big.

To change your life, you must literally change your life, the physical actions and the mindset.

Just as with success, the same goes with health.

Do you have the habit of a healthy diet and regular athletic exercises?

Healthy people have healthy habits.

If you are unhappy about your weight and figure, point the finger at your habits once again.

To become healthy, happy and wealthy, we must first become that person in the mind.

Success is all psychological.

Success has nothing to do with circumstances.

Until we have mastered the habits of our thinking we cannot project this success on the world.

We must first decide clearly who we want to be.

We must decide what our values are.

We must decide what we want to achieve.

Then we must discipline ourselves to take control of our destiny.

Once we know who we are and what we want to do,

Behaving as if it were reality becomes easy.

We must start acting the part.

That is the measure of true faith.

We must act as if we have already succeeded.

As the old saying goes: "fake it UNTIL YOU MAKE IT"

Commit yourself with unwavering faith.

Commit yourself with careful and calculated action.

You will learn the rest along the way

Every habit works towards your success or failure,

No matter how big or how small.

The more you change your approach as you fail, the better your odds become.

Your future life will be the result of your actions today.

It will be positive or negative depending on your actions now.

You will attain free-will over your thoughts and actions.

The more you take control, the happier you will be.

Guard your mind from negativity.

Your mind is your sanctuary.

Ignore the scaremongering.

Treat your mind to pure motivation.

We cannot avoid problems.

Problems are a part of life.

Take control of the situation when it arises.

Have a habit of responding with action rather than fear.

Make a habit of noticing everybody and respecting everybody.

Build positive relationships and discover new ideas.

Be strong and courageous, yet gentle and reasonable.

These are the habits of successful leaders.

Be meticulous.

Be precise.

Be focused.

Make your bed in the morning.

Follow the path of drill sergeants in the royal marines and US navy seals.

Simple yet effective,

This one habit will shift your mindset first thing as you greet the new day.

Choose to meditate.
Find a comfortable place to get in touch with your inner-self.
Make it a habit to give yourself clarity of the mind and spirit.
Visualize your goals and make them a reality in your mind.

Choose to work in a state of flow.
Be full immersed in your work rather than be distracted.
To be productive we need to have an incredible habit of staying focused.
It will pay off.
It will pay dividends.
The results will be phenomenal.

Every single thing you choose to make a habit will add up.
No matter how big or how small,
Choose wisely.

Choose the habit of treating others with respect.
Treat the cleaner the same as you would with investors and directors.
Treat the poor the same as you would with the CEO of a multi-national company.
Our habits and attitude towards ourselves and others makes up our character.

Choose a habit of co-operation over competition,

After all the only true competition is with ourselves.

It doesn't matter whether someone is doing better than us as long as we are getting better.

If someone is doing better we should learn from them.

Make it a habit of putting ourselves into someone else's shoes.

We might stand to learn a thing or two.

No habit is too big or too small.

To be happy and successful we must do our best in them all.

Chapter 16:

<u>10 Habits of Warren Buffet</u>

Warren Buffett, popularly known as the "Oracle of Omaha", is the chairman and CEO of Berkshire Hathaway and an American investor, corporate magnate, and philanthropist. He's undoubtedly a well-known investor of all time-if, not history, continuously setting records of knowledge, talent, and a strong drive to reach his future objectives. Buffett is also a supporter of leadership and personal growth, and he shares his wealth of advice to help you better your decisions.

So, how did he land to success? Here are ten warren's habits, which would you benefits later on.

1. His Reading Habit

Reading- a habit that he adheres to religiously, is one rule that Warren Buffett considers key to success. So he reads The Wall Street Journal, USA Today, and Forbes in the mornings and The Financial Times, The New York Times, Omaha World-Herald, and American Banker throughout the day.

Reading is basic to improving your understanding. Among other books, self-improvement books are popular with Buffet. That's said, consider jogging your memory with a mind-stimulating activity like reading. Engage in "500" pages book, article, newspaper each day, in the area that self-improves your interests. Reading makes you more knowledgeable than other people.

2. Compound Your Life and Finances

As per Albert Einstein, "Compound interest is the world's eighth wonder." if you understand it, you earn it; if not, you pay it." Warren Buffet's approach to investments never changes. He maintains his compounding investment principle as an investing strategy and aligns it with thinking patterns.

Compounding is the practice of reinvesting your earnings in your principal to generate an exponential return. Are you compounding your life finances, relationships, reading? That is how knowledge operates. It accumulates in the same way that compound interest does. You can accomplish it, but best when you're determined!

3. Isolation Power

Despite becoming the world's best investor and stock market trader, Warren Buffett claims that living away from Wall Street helped him. When you block the outside influence, you think quickly, distract unimportant variables and the general din.

Isolation exposes you to more prospects as it keeps you from external influence and information, making you unique and infamous.

4. Managing Your Time Wisely

You'll have 24 hours a day, or 1,440 minutes. All the leaders and successful people like Warren have one thing in common because of how powerful it is: Time management.

5. Do What You Enjoy

Your career or business may start with low returns but approaching it in Warren's way means switching your mind entirely to the job. If your mind likes something and you feed it to it regularly, it never turns off.

Working for a low salary is a momentary inconvenience, but it multiplies at the rate your skills increases, and they grow tremendously because you enjoy doing it.

6. Inner and Outer Scorecards

The key question about how people act is whether they have an Internal or an outward scorecard. So, naturally, it is preferable to be happy with your Inner Score to live a peaceful and happy life.

Having an inner scorecard is being contented with your thoughts and making decisions based on those thoughts while ignoring external influences or judgement skills. The deal is to live through values that matter to you, especially when making tough financial decisions.

7. Mimic the Finest Managers' Leadership Behaviours

Much of your life endeavours are, in most cases, shaped by the person who you choose to admire and emulate. Warren's admiration of Tom Murphy scourged him to greatness in leading his businesses to success.

8. Understand What You Have

Know and understand the companies in which you have a stake. Examine and analyze what is going on within the company, not what is going on in the marketplace.

The company's operations should be straightforward such that you can explain to an 8-year-old child how the company produces money in one phase. Familiarize enough with your investments while keeping a tab with its exact worth.

9. Invest in Your Well-Being

The basic right towards success is your well-being. Take care of your mental and physical health first, especially when you're young. The importance of life's fundamentals- nutritious diet, regular exercise, and restful sleep-is self-evident. It all boils down to whether you're doing them correctly.

10. Create a Positive Reputation

Buffett's reputation stems from his moral and level-headed attitude to both his personal and business life. You should view your business/career as a reflection of yourself, which means you should be careful and sensitive of how your decisions influence others.

Conclusion

Just as Warren, enhance your cognitive skills through learning to become more knowledgeable for bettering your life initiatives. While focusing on your major goals, take care of your mental and physical well-being. Therefore, invest your efforts and time carefully because the returns will multiply eventually.

Chapter 17:

Happy People Celebrate Other People's Success

What a phony smile... Why do people want him? How has he accomplished anything? It's ME they need. I'm the one who should be successful, not him. What a joke." This was my inner dialogue when I heard about other people's success. Like a prima donna, I seethed with jealousy and couldn't stand to hear about people doing better than me.

But all the hating got me nowhere. So I thought about who I was really mad at...it wasn't the successful people I raged at. When I got more serious about succeeding, I channeled that useless envy into accepting myself.

I practiced self-acceptance with a journal, through affirmations, and by encouraging myself—especially when I failed. Then something weird happened. I started feeling happy for other people's success. Without a hint of irony, I congratulated people on their hard work, and I applauded their success with my best wishes. It felt good. I felt more successful doing it.

"Embrace your uniqueness. Time is much too short to be living someone else's life." – Kobi Yamada

My writing career caught fire at the same time. I was published on sites that I'd only dreamt of, and whose authors I had cussed for doing things that the egotistical me still hadn't. Congratulating others started a positive feedback loop. The more I accepted myself, the more I celebrated other people's success and the more I celebrated their success, the more success I achieved. Now that I look back, I could've hacked my growth curve by celebrating others' success as a daily ritual.

1. It conditions you for your own success

Feeling good for someone else's success helps you generate the same feelings you need for your own accomplishments. So put yourself in the other's shoes. Revel in their accomplishments; think of all the hard work that went into it. Celebrate their success and know that soon you'll experience the same thing for yourself. Apply the good feelings to your visions for a brighter future.

2. You'll transcend yourself

Everyone knows that to actually succeed, you need to be part of something bigger. But most people are kept from that bigger something by wanting all the focus for themselves. it's an ego issue.

Through celebrating others, you'll practice the selflessness it takes to let go of your tiny shell and leap into the ocean of success that comes through serving others. Cheer your fellow entrepreneurs. Feel their success. Let go of your want for recognition and accept that you'll get it when you help enough other people.

Chapter 18:

Being Authentic

Today we're going to talk about the topic of authenticity. This topic is important because for many of us, we are told to put on a poker face and to act in ways that are politically correct. We are told by our parents, Teachers, and many other figures of authority to try to change who we are to fit society's norms and standards. Over time this constant act of being told to be different can end up forcing us to be someone who we are not entirely.

We start to behave in ways that are not true to ourselves. We start to act and say things that might start to appear rehearsed and fake, and we might not even notice this change until we hear whispers from colleagues or friends of friends that tell us we appear to be a little fake. On some level it isn't our fault as well, or it might be. Whatever the reason is, what we can do however is to make the effort to be more authentic.

So why do we need to be authentic? Well technically there's no one real reason that clearly defines why this is important. It actually depends on what we want to expect from others and in life in general. If we want to develop close bonds and friendships, it requires us to be honest and to be real. Our friends can tell very easily when it seems we are trying to hide something or if we are not being genuine or deceptive in the things we say. If people manage to detect that we are insincerity, they might easily choose to not be our friend or may start to distance themselves from us. If we are okay with that, then i guess being authentic is not a priority in this area.

When we choose to be authentic, we are telling the world that we are not afraid to speak our mind, that we are not afraid to be vocal of our opinions and not put on a mask to try and hide and filter how we present ourselves. Being authentic also helps people trust you more easily. When you are real with others, they tend to be real with you too. And this helps move the partnership along more quickly. Of course if this could also be a quick way to get into conflicts if one doesn't practice abit of caution in the things that they say that might be hurtful.

Being authentic builds your reputation as someone who is relatable. As humans we respond incredibly well to people who come across as genuine, kind, and always ready to help you in times of need. The more you open up to someone, they can connect with you on a much deeper emotional connection.

If you find yourself struggling with building lasting friendships, stop trying to be someone who you are not. You are not Kim Kardashian, Justin Bieber, or someone else. You are you, and you are beautiful. If there are areas of yourself you feel are lacking, work on it. But make sure you never try to hide the real you from others. You will find that life is much easier when you stop putting on a mask and just embracing and being you are meant to be all along.

Chapter 19:

<u>10 Habits of Usain Bolt</u>

Usain Bolt, fondly referred to as the fastest man alive, was born on 26th August 1986 in Jamaica. His sporting talent was discovered by his parents and teachers in his childhood. Bolt could win the 10-meter running challenges at school and he once finished a 200-meter race in 22.04 seconds.

Here are ten habits of Usain Bolt:

1. <u>He is courageous.</u>

Courage is the most noticeable trait in many people. Usain Bolt is a man of great courage from his childhood. His first major sporting event was the IAAF World Youth Championship in 2001 in Hungary when he was a teenager.

The courage of a young boy running in a world event was rare but Bolt made history by participating in the event.

2. <u>He is teachable.</u>

Bolt is a humble sportsman. The sports coach at William Knibb Memorial high school encouraged Bolt to join athletics instead of cricket. The renowned athlete took the coach's advice seriously and majored in athletics.

Usain Bolt's talent was noticeable from his childhood but he trained under the tutelage of Glen Mills. His coach sharpened his skills at the track and the young boy's star in sports shone brighter.

3.   He is a record-breaking athlete.

You can be almost sure that Bolt would set a new record in every game that Bolt participated in. He has been breaking his record in the 100-meter race. He clocked 9.72 seconds at the Reebok Grand Prix.

A few months later, he broke his record to run 9.69 seconds at the Beijing Olympics in August 2008. He set a world record in running 100 meters in 9.58 seconds at the IAAF World Championships in 2009! His record has never been broken in any official race to date.

4.   He is confident.

Bolt is a very confident man. He has exuded great confidence in himself before races and his win cemented his victory. He is dubbed the fastest man alive – a record he prides has never been broken.

He once told reporters that he went to the Olympics to win and prove that he is the best. He prides himself in putting the sport on a different level and how he wants to be among the greatest sportsmen – Mohammed Ali and Pelé.

5.   He is resilient.

Bolt has suffered injuries, recovered, and returned to the track many times. Nothing has ever put the World's fastest man down. In 2015, his pelvic muscles were injured and he had to withdraw from two races. However, in July of the same year, he made a powerful comeback to win the 100 meters race.

Before his retirement, he collapsed from a hamstring injury and his teammates helped him cross the finish line. Nevertheless, his spirit was not put off. He retired from active sports honorably with his head held high.

6. He values the privacy of his health.

The eight-time Olympic gold medalist is very careful with how he releases the status of his health to the public. He has always been open to his fans when he is injured but never releases details of his medical reports.

Some people questioned the timing of his retirement when he announced it due to a hamstring injury he had incurred in 2017 during his last race. He posted his X-ray images on Twitter showing his injury but later removed all the tweets. He retracted saying that he does not release his medical report to the public.

7. He is generous.

He donated $50,000 to victims of the Sichuan earthquake in 2008. Later in 2015, Bolt donated $1.3 million and sports equipment to his former school in Jamaica.

He yearns to reach the less privileged through the Usain Bolt Foundation. The foundation is majorly based in Jamaica where it is concerned with the welfare of the less privileged children.

8. He is strong-willed.

Usain Bolt is unshaken by the opinions of other people. He is strong-willed and lives to fulfill his dreams. He maintains his identity for who he is and no mortal comes between him and his plans.

After retiring from athletics, he contemplated joining soccer after he had recovered from his injury. He told reporters at the U.S Formula One Grand Prix that he does not care what people are going to say, he will give soccer a try.

9. He is a writer.

Besides the sports giant that people know of Usain Bolt, he is also a writer. Following his world record at the IAAF World Championships in 2009, he published the memoir *My Story: 9:58: The World's Fastest Man* the following year.

The book was reissued in 2012 as *The Fastest Man Alive: The True Story of Usain Bolt*. The following year, he authored *Faster than Light: My Autobiography*. He published all three books within three years.

10. He is private with his personal life.

It is expected that being an international figure, his personal life would be bare to the public. However, Usain Bolt has managed to keep his life private, especially his love life.

He confessed to a journalist in January 2017 that he has been dating Jamaican model Kasi Bennett for almost three years! In May 2020, the couple had their first child together. Details of Bolt's private life remain scanty.

In conclusion, these are the ten habits of the World's fastest man who is in the Guinness world records.

Chapter 20:

There's No Time for Regrets

Regret. Guilt. Shame.

These are three of the darkest emotions any human will ever experience. We all feel these things at different points in our lives, especially after making a "bad" decision. There are certain situations some of us would rewind (or delete) if we could. The reality is, however, there is an infinite number of reasons we should never regret any of the decisions we make in our lives.

Here are 7 of them:

1. Every decision allows you to take credit for creating your own life.

Decisions are not always the result of thoughtful contemplation. Some of them are made on impulse alone. Regardless of the decision, when you made it, it was something you wanted, or you would not have done it (unless someone was pointing a gun at your head).

Be willing to own the decisions you make. Be accountable for them. Take responsibility and accept them.

2. By making any decision involving your heart, you have the chance to create more love in the world by spreading yours.

Your love is a gift.

Once you decide to love, do it without reservation. By fully giving of yourself, you expand your ability to express and receive love. You have added to the goodness of our universe by revealing your heart to it.

3. By experiencing the disappointment that might come with a decision's outcome, you can propel yourself to a new level of emotional evolution.

You aren't doing yourself any favors when you try to save yourself from disappointment. Disappointment provides you with an opportunity to redefine your experiences in life. By refining your reframing skills, you increase your resilience.

4. "Bad" decisions are your opportunity to master the art of self-forgiveness.

When you make a "bad" decision, *you* are the person who is usually the hardest on yourself. Before you can accept the consequences of your decision and move on, you must forgive yourself. You won't always make perfect choices in your life. Acknowledge the beauty in your human imperfection, then move forward and on.

5. Because of the occasional misstep, you enable yourself to live a Technicolor life.

Anger. Joy. Sadness.

These emotions add pigment to your life. Without these things, you would feel soulless. Your life would be black and white.

Make your decisions with gusto. Breathe with fire. You are here to live in color.

6. Your ability to make a decision is an opportunity to exercise the freedom that is your birthright.

How would you feel if you had no say in those decisions concerning your life? Would you feel powerless? Restricted? Suffocated?

Now, focus on what it feels like to make the decisions you want to make. What do you feel? Freedom? Liberty? Independence?

What feelings do you *want* to feel?

Freedom. Liberty. Independence.

As luck would have it, the freedom you want is yours. Be thankful for it in every decision you make, "good" or "bad."

7. When you decide to result in ugly aftermath, you refine what you *do* want in your life.

It's often impossible to know what you want until you experience what you don't want. With every decision, you will experience consequences.

Use those outcomes as a jumping-off point to something different (and better) in your future.

Chapter 21:

<u>10 Habits of Roger Federer</u>

Roger Federer is a Swiss professional tennis player who has won 20 Grand Slams, sharing a record with Rafael Nadal and Novak Djokovic (The Big Three). Federer has been the world No. 1 in the ATP rankings for a total of 310 weeks, including a record 237 consecutive weeks, and has closed the year-end as No. 1 five times.

Roger Federer has achieved unprecedented success in his profession as well as in other areas of his life. He is lauded as the best tennis player of all time with his dominance play style that combines excellent footwork and shot-making abilities. He has been honoured with the Laureus World Sportsman of the Year award four times in a row. Giving a glimpse of his axioms for success, Federer shared a couple of his slogans.

Here are the ten habits of Roger Federer.

1. Hard Work

After the 2016 Wimbledon break due to knee injury, Federer come back claimed the Australian Open crown, defeating his arch-rival Rafael Nadal. His response to this excellent comeback was simple: "work the hardiest." The foundation of your career success is your consistent hard work.

2. Establish Strategic Goals

Roger Federer excels at setting both short and long-term objectives. He understands that short-term goals provide a cause for his daily habits to continue and that long-term ambitions include winning other Slams and legacy continuation. Maintain a laser-like concentration on your priorities and decline any offers that may jeopardize your long-term aspirations. Trust your long-term strategy, but keep your short-term goals intact for daily motivation.

3. Learn From the Chase

Roger Federer lives for the lessons he's learned throughout his journey. When he was young, he wanted to be the best tennis player in the world. That sparked a chase and a long journey to realize his boyhood desire. Pursue your passions with all your heart, but don't lose sight of the importance of your trip.

4. Rest Is an Important Productivity Metric

Federer usually schedules rest days following the Slams and other important tournaments. He also gets 11 to 12 hours of sleep per night. Rest is an essential aspect of Federer's career longevity. And like Federer, you may find yourself revived and ready for the next assignment after some well-deserved downtime.

5. To Evolve, Adapt

Between 2012 and 2017, Federer was overshadowed by Novak Djokovic, to whom he lost three finals. However, retiring was not near his thoughts but despite his age, he set out to become faster, stronger, and with an intensified killer instinct. As you get older, you become more concerned with quality than quantity because quantity harms the body.

6. Question Yourself Always

Success journey is complex; hence you must be willing to be your harshest critic. Federer has achieved a great deal of success because he is constantly questioning himself. His success bar is so high that he seeks out any flaw he can find and carves it out until it becomes a strength. Don't be too kind to yourself!

7. Learn New Skills

Identify the abilities you need to excel at your profession and continue enhancing those skills. For nearly two decades, Federer and his fitness coach, Pierre Paganini, worked hard from a young age to develop his fastness, a crucial quality in tennis. Well-deserved reward will come if you put in appropriate action.

8. Build on your strengths

Working on your shortcomings, according to Federer makes you a better player but does not make you dangerous. His extra focus goes on building on shots that his opponents find it hard to exploit can't exploit.

9. Maintains Cool in Stressful Situations

Roger, by now, is your role model for being calm in challenging and pressurized situations. When he was younger, he was highly emotional, frequently complaining and hurling rackets. He was wasting a lot of energy, which was preventing him from functioning well. He worked hard to improve his mental game, and he is now one of the finest mental performers in the sport.

10. Serve Others

Through the Roger Federer Foundation(RFF), Roger has been aiming to make a difference in the world by creating quality lives for underprivileged children, particularly in Africa. Just like Federer, use your platform to make the world a better place.

Conclusion

Federer is a model athlete. He dedicated almost his entire life to tennis, kept his head down, and worked diligently for decades to become the greatest player of all time. When you're good at anything, make it your primary focus.

Chapter 22:

<u>10 Habits of Steve Jobs</u>

Steven Paul Jobs was an American innovator, designer, and undoubtedly successful businessman. He is a narrative of entrepreneurial creation myth: he transformed imagination into technology and entrepreneur skills. He helped usher in an era of personal and tablet computing, smartphones, animated films, music, digital publishing, and retail outlets. Steve founder Apple in his parents' garage in 1976 was ousted in 1985, but later returned to the company to save it when it was a purge of bankruptcy; by the time of his death in 2011, he transformed it into the world's most valuable company. Even if Steve is no longer here, his legacy will live on.

Here are 10 Steve Jobs habits that are worth your attention.

1. You Can Anticipate the Future

Steve Jobs is still a living example of someone who can predict future trends. His efforts have benefited Apple, as evidenced by the company's dominance in digital sales. The iPhone has transformed the phone market by introducing a very sophisticated touch-screen phone. One way to incorporate this into your life is by imagining yourself in years to come because having a vision will help you anticipate, prepare for hurdles and overcome them.

2. Don't Let Circumstances Limit Your Life.

Master a habit of seeing the positive in every situation and creating a channel to reap its benefits. As an adoptive child, Steve may easily have despised his upbringing or perhaps indulged in undesirable activities as a teenager. Instead, Steve focused on the good; he decided to devote his efforts to technology and computing, and you know how wonderfully that turned out.

3. Find the Ideal Partner

Apple was co-founded by Steve and his partner Steve Wozniak, who greatly complemented Job's skill set. Similarly, to be successful, you must choose the ideal companion in your life. The people you surround yourself with have the power to make or break your life.

4. Don't Sell Crap

While many would argue that Apple only sells high-quality products, you can agree that the quality is the reason why they are still at the top. It is simply through the provision of high-quality products that they have devoted clients who are constantly eager to purchase.

5. Obstacles Are Masked Opportunities

Once you learn to see obstacles as hidden opportunities, you'll always find a way to get away out. During the development of the first Apple computer, Jobs and Wozniak ran out of money. Instead of surrendering,

Jobs sold his van, while Wozniak sold his graphing calculator. There is always a way when there is a will.

6. Take That Risk

Steve was willing to give up his company's products for the sake of advancement. Many CEOs would have been hesitant to develop an iPhone, knowing that it would almost certainly lead to the collapse of the iPod-but Jobs did it nonetheless. To progress, you must risk it. However, to make an informed decision, assess the risk's best and worst-case scenarios.

7. To Sell Your Idea, First Assess Whether it's Fit.

Compared to other companies, one thing unique about Steve and Apple is that Apple surprises the world with a new product that you could never have imagined. That is an example of empathy. That is seeing the world as it should be rather than as it is.

8. Redefine the Game

Rather than focusing on beating your competitors, redefine your game. Apple Inc. went from being on the verge of bankruptcy to releasing the iPhone ten years later because Steve played a computer game that other competitors didn't. While other smartphones featured physical keyboards, Apple developed touch-screen smartphones that most users preferred.

9. Explore the World and Try New Things

As an entrepreneur, traveling opens new windows and avenues. You must understand people from different places to instigate a consumerist understanding. After traveling to Ashram, India, Steve noted how it opened his mind to new market ideas in an interview.

10. Learning as a Child

According to Steve Jobs, learning is a continuous habit and an essential skill of success. Each time you learn a new thing, it reshapes your brain and enhances your focus. Consider how children approach learning in different ways. To them, it's merely a component of the exploration they utilize to confront the world around them.

Conclusion

Just like Steve Jobs, it all comes down to the initial step. If you have an idea, put it into action. It will die out if you do not start. Believe in your vision and get started.

Chapter 23:

How To Focus and Concentrate On Your Work

Today we're going to talk about a topic that I think everyone struggles with, including myself. Being able to sit in front of your computer for hours on end is not something that comes naturally to anyone, well not for me anyway.

Unfortunately, this is a skill that needs to be learned. And it is on some level crucial for our career success. So if this is something that you struggle with, then stick around for the rest of the video to learn how you can increase your level of concentration and to be more productive.

So what is focus and how do we get more of it?

The first thing we need to know is that focus is a state of mind. Without getting into too scientific terms, focus happens when our brains generate certain waves, I'm sure you've heard of alpha, theta, beta, waves. But to get to this state, we must give it some time. And the first step is to simply start sitting on your desk and practicing some deep breathing to get you prepared for that state. Close your eyes, just take some time to focus on your breath and nothing else. Feel your body calming down from a more excitable state, to one of more serenity and peace. Let go of any thoughts that come your way, whatever problems that crosses your mind, just let it flow away. If you need to take some time to do so right now, just pause the video and practice this deep breathing for yourself. For those that require a more holistic practice, you can check out my meditation link here, where you will be guided through a simple 10 min practice to get yourself in the right state of mind.

The next thing we need to know about focus is that it requires us to be free from distraction. When we get interrupted in our workflow by distractions such as buzzing from our phones, social media, by other people, or even our pets, we break the momentum that we have so painstakingly built. According to Newton's Law: The law states that as object at rest will stay at rest, an object in motion will stay in motion unless acted on by a net external force. The same principle applies to our focus, when we break that motion, it will take an equal amount of energy to get us back on track again. So to save our brains from having to work extra hard to keep you concentrated, it is vital that we eliminate all possible sources of distraction that will pull us away from the state of focus. It is best that we set aside at least 1-2 hours of our time where nothing and no one can disturb us. Do not schedule your meals or coffee break in between those times of concentration as the same principle applies to those as well.

The final thing we need to know is that focus is a muscle, and the more that we train it each day, the easier it gets for us to get into that state. I believe that focus, as with anything else, requires a daily routine for us to get into the habit of being able to switch quickly from play to work. As you train yourself to be more focused, by first being more attentive to the various nuances of how to achieve focus, it will come more naturally to us if we keep applying the same practice for 10, 20, 30 days in a row. When we make a conscious effort to keep distractions away, when we find less excuses to wander around our work place, when we make it a point that we will do our very best to stay focused each and every day, it will come as no surprise that your levels of productivity and concentration will definitely increase. Our brain's capacity for staying in that state of mind will increase as well. And hopefully we will be more creative and innovative as a result.

I want to give you one more bonus tip to help you get the ball rolling, if you find you need an extra boost. That is to think of the rewards that being focused can get you. Try your best to visualise the benefits of being productive and getting your work out of the way, the time you will have after to do the things you enjoy, if work isnt one of them. The friends that you can see after the work is done, and how much time you won't have to waste being distracted and spending your whole day in front of your computer only to realise you only put in 2 hours of actual work in. Also think of the monetary rewards maybe of being focused, how much more money you can potentially be earning, or how many clients and business deals can you close if you just became more productive. You can even think of the intrinsic rewards of being focused, how proud would you be of yourself if you had actually done the 5-6 hours of work that you promised you would do.

So for those who are struggling with focus and concentration, I challenge you to take a look at the surroundings of your workplace... What can you do to minimise the distractions, and how can you get and stay in that focused state of mind for longer without letting your concentration drift away.

I believe that you can do anything that you set your mind to. So go out there and achieve focus like never before.

Chapter 24:

<u>10 Habits of Justin Bieber</u>

Justin Drew Bieber, the Canadian singer, and songwriter was born on 1st March 1994 in Stratford, Ontario, Canada. He was raised by a single mother after his father, Jeremy, left them to start another family. Justin Bieber's mother has been instrumental in his music career. She has been his number one fan and supporter all through.

Here are ten habits of Justin Bieber:

1. <u>He is persistent.</u>

From an early age, Justin has never gotten comfortable with giving up. In 2007, he participated in a local talent competition where he was placed second. This was his first-ever audition and it did not break his love for music.

His mother posted a video of his performance on YouTube for family and friends who did not see him perform in the talent competition to watch. Despite coming in second, Justin did not give up singing and his mother uploaded homemade videos of his performance on YouTube. His persistence and mother's support made him rise to fame.

2. <u>He is collaborative.</u>

Justin Bieber is very collaborative with other singers. He has welcomed partnerships and joint music performances from every willing artist. His latest hit collaboration was with Ariana Grande when they released *Stuck with U* during the coronavirus pandemic in 2020.

He collaborated with Usher when he was under his tutelage during the start of his music career. Other singers that he has worked together with are Luis Fonsi and Daddy Yankee in *Despacito* in 2017, Nicki Minaj in *Beauty and a beat* in 2012, DJ Snake in *Let me love you,* Big Sean in *Let me love you,* and many more.

3. He is remorseful.

Justin Bieber is remorseful when he errs. Despite his good relationship with his mother during his teenage years, his relationship with his mother deteriorated for some time. He had an interview with Billboard in 2015 where he described his relationship with his mother as pretty non-existent.

He took the step of reconciling with his mother as he resolved to be a better husband to Hailey Baldwin. In 2016, Justin Bieber's mother – Pattie – confirmed that Justin had called her to wish her a happy mother's day. The two were later pictured on a holiday together and had kind words to say to each other.

4. He is social.

Justin owes his exposure to the world to YouTube. Social media has played a bigger role in putting forth his music to his fans. His YouTube channel alone has over 65 million subscribers who follow every music he releases.

He is among the most followed singers across all social media platforms; 114 million followers on Twitter and another 200 million on Instagram. His engagement with netizens is noticeable when he updates them on every project he is up to.

5. He does business.

Justin Bieber is not only a musician but also a businessman. He is estimated to be worth $285 million. He has other income streams apart from singing and songwriting.

His brand sells perfumes and nail polishes besides other merchandise. He has also done product endorsements of Calvin Klein, Proactiv, Adidas, and his clothing brand – Drew house. All these contribute to his vast business empire besides singing.

6. He does Charity.

Justin Bieber is a generous man. Despite his wealth, he has tried not to forget his humble background. He has supported 28 foundations in charity since he started doing music including The Red Cross, World Vision, Alzheimer's Association, Autism Movement Therapy, Save the Children, and many more.

In 2020, his collaboration with Ariana Grande in their song *Stuck with U* raised over $3.5million for charity to the First Responder's Children Foundation!

7. He manages scandals well.

Justin Bieber is not new to scandals. He came under global scrutiny since he was a teenager. He has achieved great accomplishments and made his fair share of mistakes. He took a public paternity test in 2011 to prove his innocence of being the father of Mariah Yeater. The results turned out negative.

2014 was a bad year for the iconic superstar. He was charged with a misdemeanor and paid $80,900 in damages, arrested twice for driving without a driving license, reckless driving, and assault. He also survived a petition from 270,000 Americans to the White House to deport him. Despite all these scandals, Justin holds his head high and continues to do music.

8. He values privacy.

Justin Bieber lives a largely public life yet he knows how to hide sections of it and only reveal them at the opportune time. Privacy is elusive to a superstar of Justin's stature.

On 7th July 2018, he secretly got engaged to his then-girlfriend, Hailey Baldwin, in an intimate and private trip to the Bahamas. Thereafter, Justin announced it to his fans through his Instagram account.

9. He loves tattoos.

Bieber is no stranger to tattoos. He has had matching tattoos with his father on their torsos during their trip to Israel. They posed topless for a photo that has circulated on social media.

Justin had a matching tattoo with his wife in 2019 done by Dr. Woo after his marriage to Hailey. The celebrity couple has been in the limelight and news about their tattoos could not escape the public.

10. He handles fame graciously.

Bieber has had his fair challenge of handling fame that he received during his teenage years. However, he has been able to manage it well and make amends where he went wrong.

Money and fame change people and they stray from the good personalities that they had. Justin has risen above all the scandals he faced. He is now a disciplined family man.

In conclusion, these are the ten habits of Justin Bieber. He is a celebrated music superstar globally and his public influence cannot be ignored.

Chapter 25:

Do The Painful Things First

There are a lot of secret recipes to be happier; one of them is; seek what's painful first. Sure, this may sound a little ironic, but you will be surprised to know that all scientific research is behind this. Behavioral scientists discovered that one of the most effective ways to create an enjoyable experience is to stack the painful parts of the experience early in the process. For example, if you're a doctor, a lawyer, accountant, etc., it's better to break bad news first and then finish with the good news. This will give the clients a more satisfying experience since you start poorly then end on a solid note instead of starting well and ending badly.

There's a couple of crucial reasons why we should do the painful things first. We know that we have limited willpower during the day, and we also know that the most painful activities or tasks are sometimes the most difficult ones. So if we complete the things we find the most difficult first, we'll be exerting less energy on less complicated activities for the rest of the day. Scientific studies show that our prefrontal cortex (creative part of the brain) is the most active the moment we wake up. At the same time, the analytical parts of our brain (the editing and proofreading parts) become more active as the day goes on.

Another reason to do the painful activities firsthand after you wake up is that you would be freed from all the distractions and tend to do these tasks more quickly. If you delay the complex tasks, it will only come back to bite you. Starting with only one task for a day can be enough, as it could lead you to achieve more of them as time goes by. Things like building a new business, losing weight, or learning a new skill require pain and slow work in the beginning to get momentum. But after some persistence, you will likely see your improvements. Behavioral psychology suggests that we're more likely to lead a happier life if we're making improvements over time. Anthony Robbins once said, "If you're not growing, you're dying."

Making slow but gradual improvements is where persistency comes in. It's going to be painful and frustrating initially, and you won't learn a new language in an instant, or your business won't thrive immediately. But when you decide to sacrifice your short-term pleasure for a future pay-off, you will get to enjoy the long-term benefits over a sustained period. Stop avoiding what's hard; embrace it for your long-term happiness.

Chapter 26:

Being Mentally Strong

Have you ever wondered why your performance in practice versus an actual test is like night and day? Or how you are able to perform so well in a mock situation but just crumble when it comes game time?

It all boils down to our mental strength.

The greatest players in sports all have one thing in common, incredibly strong beliefs in themselves that they can win no matter how difficult the circumstance. Where rivals that have the same playing ability may challenge them, they will always prevail because they know their self-worth and they never once doubt that they will lose even when facing immense external or internal pressure.

Most of us are used to facing pressure from external sources. Whether it be from people around us, online haters, or whoever they may be, that can take a toll on our ability to perform. But the greatest threat is not from those areas... it is from within. The voices in our head telling us that we are not going to win this match, that we are not going to well in this performance, that we should just give up because we are already losing by that much.

It is only when we can crush these voices that we can truly outperform our wildest abilities. Mental strength is something that we can all acquire. We just have to find a way to block out all the negativity and replace them with voices that are encouraging. to believe in ourselves that we can and will overcome any situation that life throws at us.

The next time you notice that doubts start creeping in, you need to snap yourself out of it as quickly as you can, 5 4 3 2 1. Focus on the next point, focus on the next game, focus on the next speech. Don't give yourself the time to think about what went wrong the last time. You are only as good as your present performance, not your past.

I believe that you will achieve wonderful things in life you are able to crush those negative thoughts and enhance your mental strength.

Chapter 27:

Develop A Habit of Studying

Life is a series of lessons.

Your education does not end at 16 or 18 or 21,

It has only just begun.

You are a student of life.

You are constantly learning, whether you know it or not.

You have a free will of what you learn and which direction you go.

If you develop a habit of studying areas of personal interest,

your life will head in the direction of your interests.

If you study nothing you will be forced to learn and change through

tragedy and negative circumstances.

What you concentrate on you become,

so study and concentrate on something that you want.

If you study a subject for just one hour per day, in a year you would of

studied 365 hours, making you a national expert.

If you keep it up for 5 years, that's 1825 hours , making you an

international expert, all from one hour per day.

If you commit to two hours you will half that time.

Studying is the yellow brick road to your dream life.

Through concentration and learning you will create that life.

Knowledge opens doors.

Being recognised as an expert increases pay.

Not studying keeps you were you are –

Closed doors and a stagnant income.

If you don't learn anything how can you expect to be valuable?

If you don't grow how can you expect to be paid more?

It only becomes too late to learn when you are dead;

until then the world is an open book will billions of pages.

Often what we deem impossible is in fact possible.

Often even your most lofty dreams you haven't even scratched the

surface of what you are capable of.

Taylor your study to your goal –

follow the yellow brick road of your design.

Follow the road you have built and walk toward your goals.

If you want to be successful, study success and successful people,

then learn everything you can about your chosen field.

Plan your day with a set time for your study.

I don't care how busy you claim to be,

everybody can spare 1 hour out of 24 to work on themselves.

If not , I hope you're happy where you are,

because that is about as far as you will get without learning more.

Studying is crucial to success whether it's formal

or learning from books and online material at home.

The knowledge you learn will progress you towards your dream life.

If that is not worth an hour or two per day,

then maybe you don't want it enough and that's ok.

Maybe you want something different to what you thought,

or maybe you're happy where you are.

If not, it's on you to do this —

for yourself,

for your family,

and for your partner in life.

It's up to you to create the world you want —

A world that only you know if you deserve.

You must learn the knowledge and build the dream

because the world needs your creation.

Be a keen student of life and apply its lesson

to build your future on a solid and safe foundation.

Chapter 28:

<u>10 Habits of Jack Ma</u>

It takes a special person to amass a total net worth of more than $20 billion through hard work and keeping a sense of perspective. Alibaba, one of world's largest e-commerce online platforms, Ceo and founder, Jack Ma is one of the world's wealthiest people, but his success hasn't clouded his strategic direction. Jack Ma's success habits will truly inspire you whether you are an aspiring billionaire or you're a small-business entrepreneur.

To grow his e-commerce business, Jack overcame all difficulties. He had a rough upbringing in communist China. He also failed the college admissions exams twice and was turned down by more than a dozen businesses. He had previously created two failed Internet businesses. However, the third time, Alibaba took off swiftly.

Here are 10 things you can grasps from Jack Ma success journey:

1. Giving Up is Failing

Jack Ma is one person who understands the meaning of failure, as it started in his early days. He founded two companies which terribly failed before the success of Alibaba. For Ma, giving up is failure.

Give your grind your best shot even when the struggle is real. Failing shouldn't make you give up, instead make sure you see the goal through to the end. Hardship is your learning lesson, and understanding its lessons is the key to fortune.

2. Let Your Initiative Impact on Society Positively

Ma created his vision focusing on its impactful influence on consumers. He also notes that consumer's happiness should be the end goal rather than the profits.

Let your entrepreneurial path be the reason why people's lives are improving. This results will be in long-term-positive business relationships.

3. What's Matters Is Where You Finish

Your humble beginnings shouldn't prevent you from taking chances. Your spirit, toughness, grit, and fortitude will tell whether or not you'll succeed.

What matters is whether you are putting much effort as needed and this will tell how determined you are to succeed. Dig in your heels, like Jack Ma, and give every opportunity your all.

4. Act Swiftly

According to Jack Ma, you must be extremely quick in seizing opportunities. To win in the end, you must first be off the starting line. You must also be quick to recover from and learn from mistakes. Grab an opportunity that is in your line of sight as soon as you see it and work with it before anyone else does. This will elevate you above your competitors, who are merely competent.

5. Persistence

Ma believes that leaders must be tenacious and with a clear vision. Understanding what you want and having the drive to pursue it will not only put you on the path to success, but will also inspire those around you to work hard to achieve their goals. Ma's business concept is around taking pleasure in one's job and refusing to accept no for an answer.

6. Foresightedness

A good leader, according to Jack Ma, should have foresight. As a leader, it's good that you're always one step ahead of the competition by anticipating how decisions will be implemented before others. Invest your time in developing creative strategies while intensifying a trait where you always follow a knowledge-based intuition.

7. Take a risk

Ma founded Alibaba Group, a very successful conglomerate of internet enterprises, in the face of skepticism from potential investors. The perfect time to take risks, is when you are pursuing your chosen goal path-when criticism is at its core.

8. Be Prepared to Fail

Jack Ma is no stranger to failure. He applied to college three times before being accepted. He created two unsuccessful companies before success of Alibaba. Even KFC didn't think he was a good fit.

When you give up on your first try, you are turning your life around. As probably you'll move on to something else while ending your dreams.

9. Take Chances When You're Still Young

Ma believes that if you are not wealthy by the age of 35, you have squandered your youth. Take use of your youth's vitality and imagination by succumbing to your goal and pursuing it.

Accept and learn from every opportunity that comes your way while you're still young. Grab every opportunity and make best of it by giving it your all. Your ability to pick up any job will help you develop tenancy.

10. Live life

Ma has a reputation for not taking things too seriously. Despite his hectic schedule, he always finds time to relax and enjoy life. If you work your whole life, you will undoubtedly come to regret it.

Conclusion

Jack Ma is one of most inspiring person in the world. His struggle way up and desire for wealth continues to inspire. Through his experience, Jack Ma demonstrates how as an entrepreneur, you can bring ambition to life.

Chapter 29:

<u>10 Habits of Adele</u>

There's no denying it, Adele Laurie Blue Adkins, better known as Adele is a musical legend. She is an English singer-songwriter and all-time great vocalist with excellent lyrical and passionate composing skills. Adele is one of the world's best-selling music artist, having sold over 120 million records worldwide.

With her exceptional voice and songwriting skills, the singer from a rough side of the town has captivated the hearts of millions of people. Adele got her admiration as an award-winning music legend, but moreover, there is much more from a lady who has overcome adversity to reach the top.

Here are 10 habits of Adele that will serve your learning journey.

1. It's Far From Easy

Criticism came thick and quick after Adele signed her first record deal because of her physical appearance. Many people, including Record label executives and high-profile designers publicly chastised her as "too fat" while suggesting weight loss to attract a larger fan base. Adele didn't let such criticism weigh in her talent as she unapologetically made hits after hits. Just like Adele, don't try to be anything or anyone but yourself.

2. Commitment Is Success

Despite constant pressure from the media to conform to their ludicrous notions of what women in the spotlight should look like, Adele chose her path and remained committed to being herself. This honesty is one of the attributes that Adele's fans admire. Such personality traits will breed your success.

3. It's Okay To Be Sad After a Breakup

When a relationship ends, you believe in acting tough and putting on a solid face. You're convinced on being tough to appear as you're suffering less than your ex-partners to win in some way. Adele defies expectations by telling her exes and the rest of the world about her grief without fear. She exemplifies humanity and vulnerability through her music.

4. Don't Take Life Too Seriously

It's okay to laugh at yourself or a hilarious scenario from time to time. Whether she's being teased in an interview or asked whether she wants to be a Bond Girl, Adele always respond with "Hahaha". She is quick to laugh, and her laugh is contagious.

5. Adversity Doesn't Stop Anything

Allow your pain to drive your mission. What if Adele waited till everything was back to normal before recording? All in all, people rushed to get her music, which she recorded in her misery. Every minute, every day, life happens and so should you commit to completing your projects without unconditionally.

6. Mirror Your Brand To Reflect Longevity

Say it quietly: Adele's tracks would have hit ten, twenty, or even fifty years ago. To call them timeless is a bit of a stretch. The fact may be that they're essentially personal because we believe that her music is basically from her life or personal experiences. However, Adele is always true to herself and then she sings authentically which is a formidable brand blend.

7. There Are Other Better Places Than the Spotlight

Adele doesn't constantly boost her social media presence and create "news" for constant consumption. Instead, she vanishes to do bizarre things like live and breathe and then reappears when she has something she hopes people would appreciate. It's tempting to feel the need to keep fulfilling it, but according to Adele, being true to yourself is more fulfilling.

8. Build Your Team, Not Just Yourself

When a technical issue nearly derailed her performance at Grammy Awards, Adele didn't cast an evil eye at her sound engineer. Not only did she make herself appear good by ending her performance properly, she also made her entire team look excellent. The question is, what do you do when life tosses you a curveball that you can't control?

9. Keep Going

Even when things are out of your control, it's easy to quit when everything seems to go wrong. But your perseverance will be rewarded!

10. Remember Where You Came From

Don't let your past or upbringing hold you back from achieving your goals in the future. Success is defined not by what you have as a child but by your level of commitment and work ethic over time. However, once you get there, don't forget where you come from.

Conclusion

You are characterized not by your physical appearance but by how you treat people and the words you use while communicating with everyone. Hence, just like Adele, have the confidence to pursue your aspirations. You never know where the road may take you.

Chapter 30:

<u>10 Habits of Tiger Woods</u>

Eldrick Tont Woods, professionally known as Tiger Woods, was born on 30th December 1975 in Cypress, California in the United States. He was the only child of an African American army officer father and a Thai mother.

Here are ten habits of the golf legend, Tiger Woods:

1. <u>He is a fast learner.</u>

Eldrick was nicknamed Tiger by his father, Earl, in honor of a fellow soldier he served together with. He was his mentor and teacher and taught him how to play golf since he was very young.

The boy Tiger was a fast learner and he had become conversant with the game at the age of 8 years.

2. <u>He is hardworking.</u>

Tiger Woods is a very hardworking man since his childhood. He was able to balance both sports and academics, and he secured a place at Stanford University. At the University, he won several amateur U.S. golf titles.

He turned to professional sporting in 1996 and won the U.S. Masters the following year when he was only 22 years. His hard work and devotion crowned him the youngest person and first African American to win the tournament.

3. <u>He is strong-hearted.</u>

Woods had a strong connection with his father and the news of his death in 2006 came as a shocker to the sports giant. Tiger's mentor succumbed to prostate cancer and his son eulogized him profoundly.

Tiger was strong enough to manage the pain of his loss and returned to sports where he won the PGA Championship and the British Open.

4. <u>He loves his family.</u>

Tiger treasures family time so much that he took some time off to welcome his first child with his wife on 18th June 2007. His time off was ground for good family time for the first-time parents.

He also took another break from work when they had their second child, Charlie Axel Woods on 8th February 2009. His hiatus lasted for two weeks then he returned to play championship.

5. <u>He is a fighter.</u>

Tiger has had several accidents over his sporting career. He has had to severally undergo knee reconstructive surgery and return to the field. He has also suffered back injuries and had his fourth back surgery in 2017.

He at one time sought professional help to manage medication intake for pain and a sleep disorder. He seeks to survive all the medical complications that he undergoes and nothing has shut down his love for sports.

6. <u>He is remorseful.</u>

Tiger Woods has faced infidelity questions. He was rumored to be having an affair with Rachel Uchitel but he maintained a loud silence. Reports of other mistresses Tiger had emerged and on 2nd December 2009, he publicly apologized over unspecified mistakes.

As infidelity reports against Tiger increased, he once more apologized to his fans about his infidelity and owned up to his mistake. Tiger also apologized to his family, friends, and fans after he was arrested and charged for driving under the influence in May 2017.

7. <u>He prefers quietness to talking things over.</u>

The golf legend is a man of few words especially when he is on the wrong side. He uses silence as his weapon leaving the public to speculate the truth.

Even after photographic evidence surfaced of his affair with Rachel Uchitel and Tiger's wife reportedly broke the back window of Wood's SUV, Tiger Woods kept quiet and instead opted to drop out of his charity golf tournament.

8. <u>He loves public relationships.</u>

Tiger is a man who does not shy from keeping his relationships in the public. After his divorce from his wife, he confirmed to the media that he was dating Lindsey Vonn.

He also kept his relationship with his wife public and always announced major family events. After some time, Woods announced his breakup with Vonn because their busy schedules kept them apart.

9. <u>He is honest.</u>

Tiger Woods is largely an honest man. He once lied about his mistresses before divorcing his wife. He however led a very honest life thereafter.

In October 2017, he pleaded guilty to reckless driving and agreed to enter a program for first-time offenders. It was unexpected but Tiger chose to learn his lesson the hard way.

10. <u>He knows how to nurse himself back to health after surgery.</u>

Tiger Woods is among the few sportspeople who have undergone many surgeries because of their sport. He has emerged victorious after every medical procedure he has had to go through.

After resuming playing golf from medical-related complications, Tiger has managed to secure a good position in the rankings.

In conclusion, these are ten habits of the golf legend – Tiger Woods. The 46-year-old golfer has created a name for himself in the history of the sport.

Chapter 31:

This Is Life

Who doesn't ponder the most basic and primary question, 'What is Life?' It is a bit cliche, but not unnecessary at all. And it certainly isn't illogical to think about what we are and what we have.

We often take life for granted but never realize what we have is special. We never contemplate the most important aspect of our existence.

We evolve during our time on this Earth. We start from nothing. But build towards a stronger being with greater and much better ambitions. We try to excel at everything we cross paths with. We strive towards our conscious development. We work towards our physical as well as emotional well-being.

We have a lot to live for but we rarely try to live for what matters the most. We never try to live like we have a greater purpose. Rather we try to go for petty things that might not even last for that long.

Life is short compared to what is going on around us. But we have to live it like there are unlimited seasons to come, each with its own blessings, each with its own opportunities.

We, humans, have evolved enough to be able to see beyond most plain things, but we chose to get soaked up in shallow waters. This life is a deep ocean with limits practically unpredictable.

Life is unexpected, it's unintentional, it's fussy but worth living for.

The life we see today is the collection of infinite, unbroken, and eternal events, rippling together simultaneously.

We say someone is alive when we see them breathing and moving but we never really know if that person is actually alive inside. We never really think about if the person is happy inside and enjoying what they have right now. We never try to look through the person and help them be alive for what matters.

Life never treats everyone the same way. But you don't need to get depressed every time you miss an alarm, or perform badly in an exam, or don't have the proper stats to show for your annual sales.

It doesn't always end badly and it certainly isn't bad every time of every day. It's just our psychology that makes us treat ourselves and life in a way that makes life demeaning and not worth it.

Everything is worth it once you try to look past the bad things and focus on the good ones you still get left with.

You have this one life, so go and live it like it matters the most to you. You might have to get a bit selfish and you might have to offend some people. Not deliberately, but just because you need some time and space which they might not allow, but it doesn't matter.

The epitome of life is that you have a clock ticking with each second getting you closer to the end. But you can still run around the clock and make it work as a swing. Enjoy with a purpose. Lead with your heart and you will come across wonders.

Chapter 32:

<u>10 Habits of Drake</u>

Aubrey Drake Graham, famously known as Drake, was born on 26th October 1986 in Toronto, Canada. Drake was born a musician – a trait from his family roots.

Here are ten habits of Drake:

1. <u>He Identifies Himself With His African Heritage.</u>

Although Drake was born outside Africa, he is proud of the African culture where his father hails from. In an interview, he once said that he considers himself more of a Black man than White.

He is not shy of his African descent. When sharing about his childhood, he recalls that he was raised by his mother in a Jewish setting and he felt out of place in a high school of dominant white people.

2. <u>He Loves Acting.</u>

Drake rose to fame in a teen drama series *Degrassi: The Next Generation* where he played the role of Jimmy Brooks. So great was his passion for acting that he dropped out of school to pursue acting as a career.

He starred in *Degrassi* from 2001 to 2009. This was something Drake as a teen had not envisaged in his life. He landed the acting role after his classmate's father had asked his son to have anyone who made him laugh at school audition for him.

3. <u>He Is Hardworking.</u>

The young Graham managed to build a name for himself just a year after appearing in *Degrassi*. In 2002, he bagged a young artist award. This was the beginning of his star shining brighter.

He has worked hard in his music career and won a Grammy award for the best rap album, *Take care* in 2013. His hard work has put him in a position to mingle with giants in the music industry both in America and Canada.

4. <u>He Has Thick Skin.</u>

Drake has developed a thick skin against scandals in his music career. He once had a bitter rivalry with Chris Brown as they were competing for Rihanna's love. This erupted into violence and both were sued for damages by those who were hurt in the incident.

Nothing has derailed his journey in music. He was once sued by his former girlfriend over her input in co-writing *Marvin's Room*. She was seeking credit for it but Drake managed to settle the matter out of court.

5. <u>He Is Aggressive.</u>

Drake does not take insults lying down. He responds with fire for fire. He has found himself in feuds with Tyga and Meek Mill. In 2015, Meek alleged that Drake was using a ghostwriter for a song they were collaborating.

Drake recorded and released two diss tracks aimed at Meek Mill within a single week. In the following year, he was also in another war of words with Joe Budden.

6. He Has A Strong Determination.

Drake is a strong-willed person and nothing obscures his way to success. They may only delay him but not prevent him from attaining his goals. This led him to release his famous song *Started from the bottom* in 2013 inspired by his struggle for success.

In an interview with MTV News, Drake is quoted saying that he wanted the world to know through that song that he works hard to be successful. It is not a coincidence.

7. He Speaks His Mind.

Only a day after his hit single *Hotline Bling* won a Grammy award for the best rap song in 2017, he did not mince his words to the Grammys for pushing him into the rap category. He publicly declined the award.

It is enviable how he speaks his mind without second thoughts. His outspoken nature has earned him fans and foes alike but still he soldiers on.

8. He Does Not Hold Grudges.

Drake is a man who does not keep a record of wrongs. He was on bad terms with Chris Brown when they were both competing for Rihanna's attention. It is unthinkable that they would later reunite once more.

He reconciled with Chris Brown and they released a hit song, *No Guidance* in 2019. Drake referred to Chris Brown as the most talented human being on the planet. Drake also championed Meek Mill's release from prison and celebrated Mill's release through social media.

9. He Is A Great Songwriter.

Drake knows how to either subtly or directly throw jabs to his target. His songs are always pregnant with a message for his fans.

He has answered his critics on allegations that he uses a ghostwriter for his lyrics through diss tracks. The latest is *Duppy Freestyle* aimed at rapper Pusha T in 2018.

10. He Values Family.

Drake has faced allegations from rapper Pusha T that he is a deadbeat father and he is hiding a child. The following month, Drake confirmed Pusha T's claim. He defended himself that he delayed announcing his son's birth because the paternity test was inconclusive.

However, after it was clear that Adonis was his son, Drake could not hold his joy of being a father. He gushed over the toddler and posted pictures of his nuclear family on Instagram.

In conclusion, these are the ten common habits of Drake both in his public and private life.

Chapter 33:

How To Find Your Passion

Today we're going to talk about a topic that i think many of you are interested to know about. And that is how to find your passion.

For many of us, the realities of work and obligations means that we end up doing something we dislike for the money in the hopes that it might buy us some happiness. That sometimes we stop following our passion because maybe it does not exactly pay very well. And that is a fair decision to make.

But today, i hope to be able to help you follow at least one passion project at any point in your life in the hopes that it might help elevate your spirits, give your life more meaning, and help you live each day with a renewed drive and purpose.

You see, the world can be very dull if we chase something that we actually don't really feel attracted to. For example, when we are forced to do something out of sheer dread day in and day out, it will suck the living soul out of us and we will tend to fall into the trap of running an endless wheel with no hope in sight. When we chase material things for example, money or luxury products, we sell our soul to a job that pays well physically but not emotionally and spiritually. As a human being, we have traded our very essence and time, for a piece of paper or digital currency that serves no purpose than to enrich us externally. While it might feel good to be living comfortably, past a certain threshold, there is a point of diminishing returns. And more money just doesn't bring you that much joy anymore.

Yes you may have the fanciest, car, house, and whatever physical possessions you have. But how many of you have heard stories of people who have a lot of money but end up depressed, or end up blowing it all away because they can never spend enough to satisfy their cravings for physical goods and services. What these people lacked in emotional growth, they tried to overcompensate with money. And as their inner self gets emptier and emptier, they themselves get poorer and poorer as well.

On the flip side, many would argue that passion is overrated. That passion is nothing but some imaginary thing that we tell ourselves we need to have in order to be happy. But i am here to argue that you do not need to make passion your career in order to be happy.

You see, passion is an aspiration, passion is something that excites you, passion is something that you would do even if it does not pay a single cent. That you would gladly trade your time readily for even if it meant u weren't getting anything monetary in return. Because this passion unlocks something within you that cannot be explained with being awarded physical prizes. It is the feeling that you are truly alive and happy, you are so incredibly grateful and thankful to be doing at that very moment in time, that nothing else mattered, not even sleep.

To me, and I hope you will see this too, that passion can be anything you make it out to be. It can be something as simple as a passion for singing, a passion for creating music, a passion for helping others, passion for supporting your family, passion for starting a family, passion for doing charity work, passion for supporting a cause monetarily, or even a passion for living life to the fullest and being grateful each day.

For some lucky ones, they have managed to marry their passion with their career. They have somehow made their favourite thing to do their job, and it fulfills them each day. To those people, i congratulate you and envy you.

But for the rest of us, our passion can be something we align our soul with as long as it fulfils us as well. If we have multiple mouths to feed, we can make our passion as being the breadwinner to provide for our family if it brings us joy to see them happy. If we have a day job that we hate but can't let go off for whatever reasons, we can have a passion for helping others, to use the income that we make to better the lives of others.

And for those who have free time but are not sure what to do with it, to just simply start exploring different interests and see what hobbies you resonate with. You may never know what you might discover if you did a little digging.

What I have come to realize is that passions rarely stay the same. They change as we change, they evolve over time just as we grow. And many of the passions we had when we were younger, we might outgrow them when we hit a certain age. As our priorities in life change, our passions follow along.

In my opinion, you do not need to make your passion your career in order to be truly happy.. I believe that all you need is to have at least 1 passion project at any given point of time in your life to sustain you emotionally and spiritually. Something that you can look forward to on your off days, in your time away from work, that you can pour all your time and energy into willingly without feeling that you have wasted any second. And who knows, you might feel so strongly about that passion project that you might even decide to make it your career some day. The thing is you never really know. Life is mysterious like that.

All I do know is that chasing money for the wrong reasons will never net u happiness. But having a passion, whatever it may be, will keep you grounded and alive.

So I challenge each and everyone of you today to look into your current life, and see there are any bright spots that you have neglected that you could revive and make it your passion project. Remember that passion can be anything you make out to be as long as you derive fulfilment and happiness from it. Helpfully one that isn't material or monetary.

CPSIA information can be obtained
at www.ICGtesting.com
Printed in the USA
LVHW051549140122
708430LV00013B/608

9 781804 280300